PAL

Blackpool Council

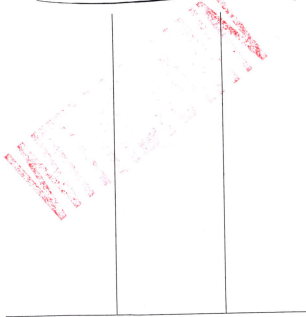

Please return/renew this item
by the last date shown.
Books may also be renewed by
phone or the Internet.

Tel: 01253 478070
www.blackpool.gov.uk

3 4114 00672 1541

MAURICE HARMON

Loose Connections

salmonpoetry

Published in 2012 by
Salmon Poetry
Cliffs of Moher, County Clare, Ireland
Website: www.salmonpoetry.com
Email: info@salmonpoetry.com

ISBN 978-1-908836-19-9

COVER ARTWORK: *Maura Harmon*
COVER DESIGN: *Siobhán Hutson*

Salmon Poetry receives financial support from The Arts Council

i.m Catherine Lynch Czekanska, 1918-2012

Acknowledgements

My thanks to the editors of the *Cork Literary Review*, *Poetry Ireland Review*, and *The SHOp* where some of these poems appeared.

'A Dog's Life' appeared in *Dogs Singing. A Tribute Anthology*, compiled and edited by Jessie Lendennie, 2010.

The two villanelles. 'My Tears Come with Me' and 'The Way We Are' have been put to music by Derek Ball as part of a longer song cycle titled *The Way We Are*.

Written for the wedding of Heather Ball and Scott Anderson 'Wedding Song' was put to music for the Breton harp by Derek Ball and performed on the occasion in January 2012.

The translation from German is of a poem by Goethe with the same title. The translations from the Galician are of untitled poems by Pilar Pallarés, Nos 1 & 2 from *Libro das devoracións*, No 3 from *Leopardo son*. They appeared in *Forked Tongues. Galician, Basque and Catalan Women's Poetry in Translation by Irish Writers*, edited by Manuela Palacios, 2012.

My thanks to the Heinrich Böll Committee who allowed me to stay in the Heinrich Böll cottage on Achill Island where several of these poems were written.

Contents

If You Want to Hear

If you want to hear how I speak, let me bring you
below the Lady's Stairs to drink from a spring
straining down through rock and up through stone,
although water alone will not slake our thirst.

We need broken shell, grit, stone
waves chasten day after day, clouds
cut loose in the winds, distractions
that only plunging cormorants own.

We need the queasiness of slabs extending
ambivalent legs out to sea, rocks that moan
when the tide recedes, depths inking
unspeakable scripts that stick and sting.

Going Away

It was not a good beginning. The arrival
at the river not good, nor the transfer
to a bus that rattled us closer to the end.

I do not remember anything we said,
can only imagine how she must have felt,
handing me over to a group in waiting.

I felt subtle enfolding, a drawing in,
the notion that they had a claim on me,
that I should become more like one of them

even though that meant leaving what I knew,
forgetting what they did not care about:
Ardgillan fields, Ardgillan strand.

None of that had any value there
in gleaming corridors, weeping walls,
where I bit my tongue day after day.

In the long run they asked too much of me
and I came back to what they did not accept –
things as they are, the script of many selves.

Croissants

In Bewley's Oriental Café
Before I even had a first sip
I saw her sitting across from me.

Her thighs in a lovely grin
Under a dark green skirt.
Black tights elegantly on view.

A wide grin to start the day.
Infectious, careless, at ease,
More bracing than choicest blend.

Finding Your Knickers in the Park

so light
they may be flicked away
with the slightest touch

let the play begin –
fore, aft, in between –
let us join

in the sport of kings
the frolic of queens
Heaven's light in our limbs

Just for Now

She did not mean to have an affair.
In any case it was impossible:
They lived on different continents.
So they were safe and for some reason
Neither understood they had a good fling,
Sex here, there, and everywhere, a few drinks,
Lunch, lots of laughs, a carefree few days.
No strings attached, this was just for now.

It was too good. They wrote. Talked on the phone,
Remembered, had a good laugh, began to consider
They might do it one more time. Definitely.
So it began, so it continued, but it was not easy.
She knew the risks – a delayed flight,
A letter mislaid, a phone call overheard.
She kept telling herself, it was just for now,
This would be the last time. Definitely.

Her New Curate

After a chance meeting at the end of the church
she began to help with parish lists, accounts,
shopping; enjoyed the fun, cups of tea,
glasses of wine, TV shows, friendship
like no other, sweet intimacy.

At Mass watched him moving the missal,
pouring wine and water, his fingers' elegance
as he raised the chalice, their trembling
when he settled the host within her palm.
She knew his presence, sweet essence.

Moisture seeping like water through moss,
control ebbing – philosophy, theology,
the shutting out, the shutting in.
This was fire, this was ice, five tastes
on the tongue, sweet consummation.

A Distant Place

As though to reconnoitre an unfamiliar place
they sometimes bring back the hazard of their fall:

she at a carefree twenty-first,
a cake, candles, gifts, then, unexpectedly,
the father offering to drive them
to a newly-opened dancehall
in a distant place;

he on a friend's snazzy bike,
roads flashing under the rims, hedges pelting past,
deciding then, on a whim,
to explore a dance-hall, newly-opened
in a distant place.

Once they met, space itself was catching.

One dance and they stayed to talk,
putting on hold the bearings of their lives.

A quick farewell, she hurrying off, and he
stretched to a wheel, holding on for dear life.

Little Woman

i

She lights the fire,
feeds the young,
lets out the hens,
draws pump water,
fills the scuttle,
makes the beds,
empties buckets,
brushes floors,
washes clothes,
scrubs flags.

ii

Starts the dinner,
chops vegetables,
washes potatoes,
sets the table,
lights the lamp,
mends clothes,
checks homework,
tells stories,
kneels with them,
prays for a happy death.

Up to the Mark

She was determined to keep him up to the mark:
Each morning straightened his tie, gave him
A freshly laundered handkerchief, made sure
He changed his socks, took in the waistband
Of his trousers, made him keep his hair trimmed,
His zipper in place and folded away.

He showed signs of confusion but these she coped with,
Smiling agreeably when he failed to remember,
Not correcting him when he got facts wrong,
Although surprised by how sure he sounded
When in truth he was all astray, listening happily
When he told stories she had heard a thousand times.

People hardly noticed his decline, he seemed
To have grown thinner, was certainly frailer,
But on the whole seemed lively enough.
His death came as a surprise. She spoke
Of its suddenness – it came out of the blue,
He had been right as rain, lively as a cricket.

It consoled her to know she had his suit pressed,
A shirt ironed, and the perfect tie for going-away.

No Mercy

You may put it behind you
for the best of motives,
or what you think are the best.

That does not mean
it is gone forever.
It will come back.

Will take you on the hop,
sleeping, or in sudden attack.
Murder, they say, will out.

So will love, so will loss.
What you thought safely hidden
shows no mercy.

Sleeping dogs lie
but sooner or later start
snapping at your heart.

Uncle Peter

The toys are ready — doll, teddy bear, rocking horse —
yet she is anxious when the doctor
closes the door and forces the air away.
Although he sits her on his lap,
chats about home, school, friends,
holds her close, is comforting,
she finds it hard to talk to this man
who knows so much about people.
Tells him about the stomach pain,
hears concern in his voice,
as he urges her to relax:
Let Uncle Peter take care of you, he whispers,
explaining that while some psychiatrists
use a strawberries-and-cream approach,
pouring lots of the white stuff into the bowl,
he encourages the body to heal itself
by activating its natural defences.
Her belt, he says, is too tight;
they should loosen it.
Undoing the clasp, he slides the zipper slowly down,
as far as it will go.
His voice is soothing,
as though the hand moving inside her knickers is not his.
But his palm is warm,
his voice calm, fingers light.
He murmurs, kisses the side of her face
— more daddy than doctor —
while fingers wear away her cares.

Into Thy Hands

His first time
He does what he has been taught
Walks slowly out to the altar
Gets every response right
Presents water and wine
As blessed hands lift a translucent host
Sounds the bell for quiet veneration:
Body of Christ.

Following the celebrant back to the vestry
To assist with the disrobing
He knows he has done as he has been taught
With a hymn of praise the priest draws him close
And sliding a hand inside the short pants
Brings godlike flesh
To mute avowal:
Body of Christ.

Although this is the first time
When the rite gets underway
He does as he has been taught
Anointed fingers show what not to do
A blameless tongue lies through his teeth
Stripped of his garments
A bitter sponge affronts skin and bone:
Body of Christ.

On Keel Strand

I watch as you push a stroller along the strand –
Your black hair and slim shape – but what I see
Is the small child who lags behind, in blue shorts,
Pink shirt, and hat, absorbed, sometimes stopping
To choose a shell or coloured stone, sometimes running
To catch up, his entire being shimmering beside the sea.

He could be on a different strand, before the war,
Before the sundering. I want to say, be good to him,
Spread your arms, do not be slow to show how you feel
Before the ubiquitous beast will surge out of the sea,
Water gushing from head and back, down straining thighs.
Where such fears come from I do not know, charging

The dark, lurking at the turn, crouched on the landing,
Every step treacherous as shifting sod or sinking
Sand, tales I heard or overheard, stories read
Or half-read, Big Foot reaching into a girl's room,
The grinning wolf in grandmother's bed,
Innocence burst before we even know it.

I want to say, don't be sanguine, don't feel safe.
Walk the long beach where raveling waves compose
a fabled narrative by day, only to unwind it again
in the long night. Let a spell be woven here.
Stretch your arms wide as you can, as often as you dare.
On this day let him feel the power of love that will not save.

Loose Connections

I have driven through the night
to find you huddled at the fire
in the same old cords.

I hear rain hammering.
Somewhere water slops
over a damaged gutter.

We began life in the same field.
You had a fair to middling left foot
and good hands but gave it up.

We took different paths.
Never a sundering, more a drifting
based on some interior strain.

Yours hidden from me, mine of no interest to you.
I sent you bits of news, you hardly noticed.
My books could end up on the floor

Or flung to the back of a shelf. That
was never an issue. Something
to talk about, to joke about.

All you read are sports pages,
pictures. Now I watch
your eyes dissolve behind glasses.

Fallen memories, loose connections.
As we part your hand grips mine
for one fierce confusing hold.

I hear rain pounding the car
and wonder why I come this far
when all I get is a broken world.

Let Us Now Praise Famous Men

Outside the church
At Seán O Suilleabháin's funeral
They were all there.

I remarked to Tomás O Con Cheanainn,
'There's no knowing what gets lost
When someone like Seán dies'.

He replied, immediately,
'And when Eugene O'Curry died,
And his father'.

The day fell back.

In a Bookshop

i.m. Patrick Lynch

We are like figures in a play
when a rising curtain
reveals a bookshop
in brilliant light.

Seeing you enter left
I go to meet you. We talk.
You invite me to meet again,
but I realise I am not free.

Knowing you will vanish
I begin to weep,
and cry out, 'Don't leave',

but the curtain
brings back the dark.

Speed

The speed of light is not a universal constant:
in the collision corridors of Cern particles are found
that go quicker;
gamma-ray emissions from the Crab pulsar
are also niftier.
In whom can we trust when Einstein lets us down?

Hanging by a Thread

Each year they take up residence
not with the openness of swallows
bending back to where they had been
under eaves and lofts
nor of Brent geese
splashing down in wetlands.
These are secret invaders.

A touch upon your face tells
of occupation in the night, nettings
in shrubs and trees, intricacies of mesh,
silent lures.

You find droopy hammocks
suspended from ceilings,
hides among bottles of wine,
chalk contagion, husks.

Bees humming for warm life
knocking against a see-through ceiling,
get caught in sticky thread,
buzz, bluster,
go quickly in the end.

Big ones, black and scary, lurk
where you least expect them
and when you see them they see you,
disappear to lie elsewhere,
with sinister intent,
foulers of marsh and fen.

I think of all-out attack,
cracks sealed, holes plugged,
the floor cemented wall to wall,
but nothing works,
nothing cuts them off,
once and for all.

The Cottage

Below Slievemore's shroud
windows turn inward to emptiness.
I do not meet a soul upon the road.

Below my room sheep cry
with the despondency of lost birds.
Footsteps of the dead scrape the floor.

A Ditch in Dugort

The stream below the bank slips over stones,
racing towards bright water, sounding off
through nettle clump and bramble hatch,
at times so hidden I do not hear it,
hear so little I wonder where everyone is,
have I the place to myself, just me,
haphazard fields and the crazy paving of the gorse?

No violence will be done to man or beast
on this June morning, where the sun
plays ring-a-ring-a-rosy with reflection,
fuchsia legs it through the hedge,
hangs fire unashamedly above yellow iris
waving back along the ditch,
while lilies keep an altar-quiet at the edge.

Such plenitude – buttercup, daisy, bramble, briar,
roses mad for kissing, shaggy thistles, vetch,
blackheads threatening me with nasal twitch,
rhododendron everywhere – in double ditches,
with lipstick on, plump and ecstatic in the hedge,
flaunting petticoats far as the eye can follow –
while bog-cotton keeps a low profile, marking time.

Hill of Howth

I am watching a young rabbit at the edge of the world
intent at green shoots,
in tune as she wrinkles her nose
with gulls serenely turning in upon themselves
and fresh, translucent growth.

We have come by tram surging
beyond field and plot to dreamy verge,
excitement beating like a pedal note,
the hill clearing its resonant head,
a lark ascending to perfect pitch

which holds more than we can know,
offbeat themes, secret correspondences;
untutored still in the scales of feeling
we give ourselves to each moment's overture,
intimation, harmony, make-believe, rests.

We do not think this day will ever stop
as we make our way down in dazed tempo,
a motif that spools away
through all that ebbs and flows
from this legendary mound.

Wedding Song

We trim the shrubs, revealing
ranks of berries, fresh and red,
robin, blue tit, blackbird, wren
compose an eager gathering.

Though air is cold, the breeze is light
And girls are dancing with delight

At once the robin comes to view,
sits near while someone clears
the earth, removes the weeds,
and lets the flowers appear.

Though air is cold, the breeze is light
And girls are dancing with delight

Blue tits feed in radiant pairs,
we empty the old, put in the new.
A blackbird takes the water, spreading
his wings, his beak still glistening.

Though air is cold, the breeze is light
And girls are dancing with delight

The wren turns up his tail in glee,
he need not fear an icy wind,
the guests arrive, a merry band,
the couple enters hand in hand.

Though air is cold, the breeze is light
And girls are dancing with delight

O pluck the strings of the Breton harp,
let voices share this wedding song,
robin, blue tit, blackbird, wren
come join this happy throng.

Term Time

Suddenly it hits me: an evening class!
I search for a student list, notes, records,
look under piles of paper, in boxes, drawers.
with no idea where to focus, seize a file,
try to remember the name of the course.
To appear alert and on top of things
apologise at once for being late.

I remember to talk about theses,
begin to go on about this, but
suddenly, it hits me:
I am in a dream, like ones I used to have –

the time I entered a classroom to
lecture on W.B. Yeats's *The Green Helmet*
and faced a group of indistinct figures
who busied themselves
with Bunsen burners, scales, smoking dishes;

the time I was handed the wrong class list
and had to hurry off to Administration
where a blur behind a hatch,
could not find the right one,
when I got back the class had gone.

I remind myself: no longer have to worry.
Yet even though awake, and in the clear,
go back over things, panic, muddle,
strangers, murky figures, struggles.

Today I want to let fly, walk backwards
with the dog, reverse smartly down the street,
fling All-Bran and Muesli to the birds,
hear them sing! hear them warble! hear them trill! –

on this day of days let openings begin,
unlock the nuns, release the monks,
put bishops on their hunkers scrubbing floors,
the Pope fixing hinges on his pope-mobile,
politicians biting one another's tongues,
as winds of change go through them like a dose of salts,

The Professor Is Relieved

In the morning
chaired a panel discussion
on feminist criticism

after that stayed in the bar
until his host drove him home
gave him a nightcap, put him to bed

all was well until
a call of nature stirred him
he found a door, found relief

where skirts, dresses, blouses,
slippers, sandals, shoes, high heels,
sighed in disbelief

Last Flight to Lanzarote
or Captain Irresolute and the Surly Crew

When exactly the outcome became inevitable is not clear,
take-off delayed for six hours,
long silences between explanations,
the captain's weaknesses exposed.

His explanation for the first delay is inadequate –

I did not know there were letters and parcels in the hold,
they will have to be removed,
before your luggage can be brought on board.

He wants us to think this delay
is not his fault but where is his authority? –

I did not know it would take so long to clear the hold;
because of this delay
we have lost our place in the queue,
and have to wait our turn.

The cabin crew starts to falter.
Sounding bossy and anxious,
they order us not to leave our seats.

The captain's next explanation –

An incoming plane has skidded on the runway
which will have to be cleared before we can leave –

makes sense until the plane beside us taxies away.

Since there has been no fresh snow
we question his next excuse –

Snow has to be cleared from the runway
which will then have to be tested for braking.

The crew refuses to give us food
until we are airborne
but now allows us to move about,
which means only one thing.

They complain about the delays,
one weeps openly:
she has to cook Christmas dinner,
fears she may not get back in time.

Like choric figures,
they talk and gesticulate with odd intensity
but will not speak to us.
When I request food for my wife,
they want to know if she is diabetic.

The captain finds reasons for more delay –

The wings have iced over,
we have to wait for the de-icing truck,
we are not first in line; other flights have priority.

His next excuse makes him seem not only helpless
but calculating –

We have been waiting so long,
with the engine running,
we do not have enough fuel;
I have difficulty getting through to the office,
they have difficulty getting through to the oilman,
and we have to wait our turn.

He must have known this for some time
and could have filled the tank already.
When the tanker appears, we cheer
in foolish anticipation,
but are not leaving.

The captain has lost –

The crew has almost reached the limit
of their working hours and cannot be asked
to work any longer; for the first time
in twenty-three years I have to cancel a flight.

We are abandoned.

When he turns off the lights
a thin band of green appears along the aisle.
We hear him trying to speak to the tower
but there is no reply.

Huddling at the front, the crew
expects steps to be wheeled to the door
but there are no steps.

Damaged Goods

These days a wind from the Azores
draws a warm breath about the house.

Fruit flies rise from a dish of grapes.
Impossible to catch, they lift away from feeble swipes.

Tinged by our mortality the grapes
are turning brown, oozing where they lie.
I pluck the bad but cannot stop the rot.

Bananas blacken and should be eaten
but I cannot bring myself to make a move.

Today's bread has signs of contamination.
I want to slice away bits of blue
and toast the rest, but caution stays my hand.

Politicians have not escaped this slow contagion.
Across the land apartments stand idly by.
Estates rattle their frames like begging bowls.

Nobody wants a derelict site where weeds
jump up in gardens never planted and pathways
crack and crumble out from the hall door.

Greed has lodged in the minds of bankers.
Speculators who have put us all in debt
will not bring themselves to show remorse.

Prelates fly over our heads
to bow above a yellow palm while we are left
to draw breath in a wind from the Azores.

TDs on Toast

Because I am distracted
by politicians in word-tangle,
pros, dodge, fudge, cons,
my toast smokes and burns.

I take the acrid slices through the hall,
fling them out for the birds,
and see them swerve, skim, shy
through a shimmer of morning light.

All strut and preen, a magpie
dives onto the grass, pecks
fast, strikes hard, but the bread
flops about, bounces over his head.

A pigeon floats down from the sky,
takes his place, pecks with ease,
with confidence, knows
he has no fear of beak or claw.

Bothered still by reek, fume
and labyrinthine squabble,
I note their nimble stepping aside
from muddle and smother.

A Dog's Life

A chip in your neck to keep you safe, a cut
In your belly to make you barren. You have
Never hunted, known the fear that clings
To rat and weasel, fought feral cats
In the woods, known the stench
Of spent cartridge, or suffered abuse
At the hands of anyone. Curbs, collars, checks, and leads
A big dog in the city: dry food from a plastic bag
A bed in the kitchen, the run of the house at night
Rewards, treats, praise, in the approved approach.
We raise you like a Spock child, no wonder
You are nervous, highly strung, behave
Like top dog, that's why I crack the whip
Secure the lead every time we go for a walk.

Tiny, the bitch, fair-haired and compact
Sat in my pram, without being told, protected me.
I knew fear for the first time when they dragged
A tape worm from her gut, spread it wet and glistening
Along the hedge, sign for days of something ugly.
I was drawn to it, puzzled by such filthy growth.
We had chased two weasels in that hedge, back and forth
In fierce engagement, the bitch yapping viciously.
When a hunted rat faced me, his back to a tree
I went cold, imagined sharp teeth on bare legs
Or the open mouth ripping my face, but Tiny raced in.
When pups were born she growled at me but after
She went for food I saw them, the helpless newborn.
As soon as their eyes opened she let me play with them.

Hector, her pup, was tireless and fierce.
Ratter, fox-hunter, rabbit-catcher, retriever
Of sticks thrown in pond and sea, with me
When I roamed fields and woods, with us

When we walked to the postman's gate
Magical place where stories grew from what we knew
A voice spoke from a fallen stump, where I was told
A knot would wink if I looked it straight in the eye.
Every Sunday we made the rounds of Hampton fields
Hunting rabbits in bushes along the railway lines.
We knew the best places, warrens, burrows
Tasty hollows, up to the hills, then back
To the yellow chimneys, the diamond panes
Where the dog got his reward, dinner's
Scraps, while we had tea, toast, and idle chat.

I know, old girl, you fret and fume, on edge
In streets, reactive and protective, if I leave you alone
A danger to head patters, dog cooers, pushy kids.
I have to take you on a lead when my instinct is
To let you run ahead, to explore the margins
But you have no fear of crossing the road
Will lope over to sniff at plastic bags, bottles, smelly spots.
In the park you are yourself, I love the way you
Prance away, strike off through the field
Play catch as catch can with swallows skimming
Your back then zooming up and away, preparing the next attack
Where the white tip of your tail waves back and forth
Where white chest and paws shine in the sun.
Oh, my beautiful girl, you will love Ardgillan,
No restraints, no rules, nothing to hedge you in.
We do not take to curbs, masters, and institutions.
We need a big sky, love, the startled imagination.

Who Goes There?

I may have felt like someone when the taxi
Dropped me off, but as soon as I give my name
At the desk I am processed to anonymity.

Name, sex, date of birth, and a number affixed
To my left wrist; then checked and double-checked.
Having unnamed me at the start they now struggle

To be certain they have the right man, before
They wheel me away and lay me down, before
A priestess in a green gown admires my dilation.

I am readied for the steely encounter, the eye identified
Wrist-band checked, entries checked, yes, the right.
For Heaven's sake, it has a black mark over it!

No wonder I talk in my sleep as she takes one lens away
And puts another in, exact positioning, smiling to herself
As I blab away. Don't mind me, my mind's astray.

     ii

Detail, dazzle, the pattern on the dinner plate
In unremembered vividness, the carpet so careworn
I was about to throw it out; its spirals now

Affirm where I come from; spines in the study
Tell me who I am: not Richard, Tom, or John but me.
Through one eye the world as it was in the beginning:

The garden greener than I thought: lilac and laburnum
High above the fence, the robin's eye alert, tiny beak
Sharp as a pin, and shining from the back of the house

To the fish pond, the garden hose a sinewy snake.
On chimneys far away cowls gleam like lurking Saracens.
Hanging baskets flown direct from Madagascar.

These alterations give me a fresh start.
I yield once again to renewals
Of the inner eye: detail, dazzle, and dilation.

The Angel

from the German

i

In childhood's early days
I often heard talk of angels
who would give up Heaven's high delights
for the Earth's sun.

So when a perplexed, anxious heart
yearns in secret, hidden from the world,
and wants unseen to bleed away in peace,
to wear away in an oozing of tears

when its prayer ardently
begs solely for deliverance,
then down an angel sweeps
and gently raises it to Heaven.

An angel has definitely come down
and on radiant wings
lifts me far from every pain –
my soul flies heavenwards!

ii

Churning, racing wheel of time
who measures out eternity;
shining spheres in outer space
who circle the orb of the world;
timeless creation, hold your horses
enough of motion, leave me be.

Bring to an end, engendering powers
the primal thoughts you constantly conceive;

control your breathing, hold your urge
be silent now just for a second;
surging pulses, curb your pounding
cease the unending day of confirmation
so that in sweet and happy oblivion
I may savour all my blessings.

When in bliss one eye another finds
and one soul in another is totally absorbed,
one being in another finds itself again
and the hope of each is fully satisfied,
when lips are silent in astonished peace,
then humans know eternity's sign
and plumb your riddle, holy nature.

iii

High-domed crests of leaves,
canopies of green,
offspring of far-off zones,
tell me, why do you complain?

Silently you bend your limbs,
make shapes in the air,
while the dumb witness to your pain
– a sweet aroma – rises.

Wide in fervent longing
you open out your arms
and clasp in crazed delusion
the barren, futile, desolate void.

Well I know, poor plants,
a destiny we share,
although suffused in light and lustre
our home is not here.

How willingly the sun departs
from the bleak light of day,
he hides himself who truly suffers
in the darkness of silence.

It becomes still, a whispered rustling
anxiously fills the dark room.
I see heavy drops suspended
from the green hem of the leaves.

iv

Sun, every evening you make
your beautiful eyes red,
when bathing at sea-level
you are taken by early death.

Yet you ascend in ancient grandeur,
glory of the gloomy world,
freshly awakened in the morning,
like a haughty, winning champion.

So why should I complain?
Why, my heart, are you so down,
if the sun itself must lose heart,
if the sun itself must sink?

If death gives birth to life
and grief brings only joy,
how grateful am I then
that nature gives such pain!

V

Tell me, what glorious dreams
embrace my senses
that have not like empty foam
worn off in dreary nothingness?

Dreams which with every hour
every day, bloom more brightly
and with heavenly bulletins
move blissfully through my heart.

Dreams which like sublime rays
are immersed in the soul
there to shape an everlasting image
neglectful of all, thinking only of one.

Dreams which when the sun in spring
warms the flowers out of the snow,
in that unexpected rapture,
welcome the new day.

So that they grow, so that they thrive
and dreaming, releasing fragrance,
expire softly on your breast,
then descend into the tomb.

My Tears Come with Me

My tears come with me everywhere I go,
At the ready should the need arise;
I never know when they may have to flow.

Old friends I have, increasingly let go,
Leaving a gap that nothing can disguise;
My tears come with me everywhere I go.

The middle-aged are not the first to know
When they are taken in a strict surprise;
I never know when they may have to flow.

The young and innocent are brought so low
The May procession seems a thing of lies;
My tears come with me everywhere I go.

The barren trees standing in a row
Are sentinels who do not close their eyes;
I never know when they may have to flow.

There must be reasons why the seasons go,
Why old and young succumb to slackening ties;
My tears come with me everywhere I go,
I never know when they may have to flow.

The Stunning Place

In the arid reaches of the night
I hear the unmistakable plod,
subdued whinnying, and know
they come by river valley, hillside track,
laneway, footpath, towpath
in grievous, imperturbable pacing,
to wait at the stunning place.

They wait for night to come,
clouds to move, stars to show,
the moon to throw its mitigating shaft
across land and sea. Some been fed sugar lumps,
dipped heads in grainy bags, lain down in green pastures;
others have risked excitements of the track,
crowds, cheers, the headlong gallop,
ear-pulling, adulation of the winner's enclosure;
work horses went back and forth
to gruff commands, were brushed, fed,
watered, stalled for the night;
some have marks of affliction,
stripes, sores, galling, their ribs unbearable.

All know when it is time
to leave the chores, forego razzle-dazzle,
lose touch with the known hand,
forget tears on the hero's chest,
move by ancient tracks
through gaps and broken walls
into the field, up to the gate, to wait.

I have seen where they pause
beside a stream, to lower
magnificent heads, drink
deep from silver streams,

relax, ruminate —
not such a bad old life,
wear and tear, ups and downs,
foals born, raised, the odd row,
kicking, biting, pawing the earth,
feel-good canters, nuzzlings.
At the gate the ground is hard
from many hooves, or soft
and muddy from many hooves,
hard, soft, makes no difference here.

In the arid reaches of the night
I hear the unmistakable plod,
subdued whinnying, and know
they come by river valley, hillside track,
laneway, footpath, towpath
in grievous, imperturbable pacing,
here to the stunning place.

The Way We Are

Last year we had so much ice and snow
this year we live in anxious expectation
not knowing what winter may bestow.

Autumn has put on a brilliant show
but we are fearful for our situation
suspicious when berries redden row upon row.

We doubt that Nature's munificence also
may affirm we need have no hesitation
in enjoying without quibble what that shows.

We make provision for a future never slow
to bring affliction on those in anticipation
of worse to come when all will be brought low.

So determined to be ready for what winter sows
we cannot find the slightest consolation
and spend our days preparing for snow.

Men praise the golden mean as though
the human race can ever know remission.
Last year we had our fill of ice and snow
this year foresee further desolation.

Putting the Clock Back

These days, Old Man, you come to mind,
as I prepare the garden for its winter slump,

things you did, sayings you had, your habit
of crossing yourself − 'now, in the name of God';
quoting a man who worked with you − 'this won't buy
the baby a new dress'− but most of all the way you
prepared and handled implements, then made them clean.

I meet you as I struggle on the ladder, or find it hard to clip
the top of the hedge, you weakened but I hardly noticed.
What do we know of ageing when the blood pounds
what do we know of old men's thoughts when ours are strong?
These are things we do not talk about, not then, not now.

Your son was blind, Old Man, never sick in your life
until the surgeon said too late and sent you home
to get it over, as you did, sinking in bad light, shadows
devouring, making it hard to see if you were still alive.

How you felt I never knew. Wrenched away
And so unused to speak, I had no words.
So off I went. You were not the kind to write.
Nor did I. The odd return never
Put things right. At odds before, and still.

When my son went off to do what he had to do
I stood still, thinking he would come back.
But he stayed, lived his life. I understood.
Even approved. Now I know the truth:
We will never take up where we left off.

These days, Old Man, I meet you on the path
see you working with the scythe, strong wrists, eagle back.
Be with me, Old Man, as I prepare for winter's slump.

Is the Mountain Out?

I know that mountain, used to watch for it,
mystified, through low cloud or dragging rain
that would cover the entire western state
from the Cascades to the Pacific coast;
then one morning as I walked the trail
to take my place before a freshman class
I saw it like a monstrance held up high
above the world, sighted through double firs.
Soaring, made real, chaste as Moby Dick.

It stayed for days, constant when we looked,
until one morning it had gone again,
shielded by clouds that had rolled over
Corvallis and Clackamas, choking the Gorge,
and I was asked, 'Is the mountain out?'
as though it were a jack-in-the-box, some toy
that could be shown from time to time, a game
that we could play, or an unreliable being
liable to come and go of its own accord.

I too began to attend its visitations
and would ask in turn, 'Is the mountain out?'
as though its presence, high above our world
of mist and snow, would affirm a reality
eternally present, although often out of sight
and indifferent to our questioning.

This weekend I know you are on the ridge
above the snowline, above Timberline Lodge,
have gone in search once more of that bright source
have walked on the glacier fields where ice
is razor sharp, have gone above the clouds
heart and lungs straining in pure air
that keeps you alert and ever on your toes
moving slowly upward step by step.

Not This Way, Love

Not this way, love, not this:
Not cast aside without regard
With a fiery dragon flaming through the air
And a greeny creature wailing in the mist.

Not this way, love, not this:
Not fitted and trussed to a bare board
With stringent earmuffs clamped against your hair
And a salvaged shoe slotted into my fist.

Not this way, love, not this:
Not seven hours beneath the glare
With your garments rent, your neck in a vice
And all our hearts held by a doubting specialist.

Not this way, love, not this.
When the charioteer declares
Let it be otherwise, let it be civil,
Not this way love, not this.

3 Poems
from the Galician

No 1

Sieved substance of morning
filled with light
made fruitful in the colour of terracotta.
Of unknown lineage,
nameless.
Deprived of history and signs
it is you alone that ponders,
given up to possession
and pillage

At the heart of now, absence.
In the blue and ochre fullness of these paths
a hollowness of soul,
a longing to be both
content and shell
to empty being like a tomb
"*dulcissima et inocentissima*"
old and little dead one, Chrisogone.

Drain myself of being for the entire span
at the whim of each instant.
Consume the past.
Tear up and wear down to reach the core
Of hardness, the necessary bones,
the nub of my nothingness.
Be centre and surface.
Let the phases of flint and anthracite
reduce the heat of my mouth,
let each bird forget me.

Place of loss.
Not even the dust shower of your bones
the coin that pays for this your dwelling place,
the joint of the crab that lodged
in the fold of cloth
along the course of waters.
Only this stillness prevails,
this porous rock that failed to hold you.

At the end of the vacuum your name.
At the end of my nothingness night
with its furious waves.
Without a pause, something goes by, singing,
leaving a high-pitched note in what the blood recalls.

No 2

that is how it is and so be it
while I heave myself through this immense afternoon
and a sundial deceives me five fifteen

how can I measure what I lose?
the missing feel of stone?
simulations of light
guarding the lifeless body of the chrysalis.

this hour does not pass:
shifts towards a less reliable edge
pants exhausted bites the heart of the wave
dawdles in the guts of whales
drags weed and gills
returns endlessly with the violet spirits of drowned women
with my wan face of twenty-odd years

how can I measure what I lose?
the irresistible pull of what I gain
in the dense waters of this hour
in the silt of what I have been, what floods through me
and drenches my being with my dead

Clay of memory
all and nothing
salt shapes the afternoon begets

No. 3

Desire, a lightning strike
lifted us as one towards a blood-red sky
torn by a bolt

Stars which had flesh
and breath
sought a foothold in the abyss.

We were stuck in the pain and stain of charts.
A spotless space,
a vast savannah waiting to be inscribed,

We mumbled words no one heard.
We were young bloods, and they faded
without finding earth.

We came down at dawn
on opposite sides of life's frontier.

The Light of Day

i

We come and go, boxed-up,
a week goes by without a word
to next-door man.

In the day's acuity
we see more clearly
what we have come to.

When the red glow went
we should have found
a different mark.

Once crossed by water
children fear no more
what lies behind the lamp.

Turn the cup down,
put candles out,
the dark will do.

ii

Distant children
make endless separations,
phone calls hold the line
until it breaks, at our end.

Comedians on the edge
work crowds to death,
next day we speak as though
we had seen *King Lear* or *Ubu Roi*.

No need to hope, or fear, or pray,
we are too far gone; what we hear
confirms what lies elsewhere
is more of the same.

Next year just another year,
turn the cup down,
let the red glow disappear,
put candles out.

The Old Let-down

It is in words we fail
unable to measure up

writing a letter I ask
does it come clean

if I read a poem
words pulse across the page

as though they no longer
lie from left to right

once I put down even
an approximation of what

I see, hear, feel, imagine
words like slow learners

falter and fail
hindering disclosure

between what I see
and what I write

the old let-down.

MAURICE HARMON, a well-known critic, scholar and academic, has written studies of writers from William Carleton to Mary Lavin and Seán O'Faolain, from Austin Clarke and Thomas Kinsella to John F. Deane, Peter Fallon, and Dennis O'Driscoll. His pioneering anthology *Irish Poetry after Yeats* appeared in 1978. His reputation as a poet has grown, particularly with the publication of his acclaimed *When Love Is Not Enough: New and Selected Poems* (Salmon, 2010), which shows the range and variety of his work. His *Dialogue of the Ancients of Ireland*, a translation of *Acallam na Senórach*, the medieval compendium of poems and stories, was published in 2009.